Confidence

Increase your Confidence and Create Indestructible, Dynamic, Potent Self Esteem to Overcome Any Challenge & Achieve Your Dreams

Robert S. Lee

Contents

Introduction 8

Chapter 1. Assess Faults Realistically 14

Chapter 2. Do Daily Affirmations 28

Chapter 3. Build a Little Each Day 40

Chapter 4. Realize Your Strengths 54

Chapter 5. Track Your Progress 68

Conclusion 76

© **Copyright 2019 by Robert S. Lee- All rights reserved.**

This document is geared toward providing exact and reliable information in regard to the topic and issue covered. The publication is sold with the idea that the publisher is not required to render accounting, officially permitted, or otherwise, qualified services. If advice is necessary, legal or professional, a practiced individual in the profession should be ordered.

- From a Declaration of Principles which was accepted and approved equally by a Committee of the American Bar Association and a Committee of Publishers and Associations.

In no way is it legal to reproduce, duplicate, or transmit any part of this document in either electronic means or in printed format. Recording of this publication is strictly prohibited and any storage of this document is not allowed unless with written permission from the publisher. All rights reserved.

The information provided herein is stated to be truthful and consistent, in that any liability, in terms of inattention or otherwise, by any usage or abuse of any policies, processes, or directions contained within is the solitary and utter responsibility of the recipient reader. Under no circumstances will any legal responsibility or blame be held against the publisher for any reparation, damages, or monetary loss due to the information herein, either directly or indirectly.

Respective authors own all copyrights not held by the publisher.

The information herein is offered for informational purposes solely, and is universal as so. The presentation of the information is without contract or any type of guarantee assurance.

The trademarks that are used are without any consent, and the publication of the trademark is without permission or backing by the trademark owner. All trademarks and brands within this book are for clarifying purposes only and are the owned by the owners themselves, not affiliated with this document.

Introduction

Confidence is key to most of life's endeavors. Whether you are trying to better your dating life, land a new job, or simply learn to be happy and content with who you are as a person, you are going to want to tackle everything with the most confident mindset that you are able to muster.

Unfortunately, this can prove to be much trickier than it may seem like it should be. Some people may suffer from emotional disturbances such as anxiety or depression. Others may be fine from a clinical standpoint, yet still possess little in the way of self-esteem due to various issues such as body weight or simply the weight of past failures. However, that does not mean one is unable to build confidence if they simply maintain the willpower to try. One must be open-minded to new ways of thinking. Above all, they must be honest with themselves. Everyone has faults, but no one should ever believe that they do not deserve to get the most out of life.

The following tips are some basic suggestions that might help a person to develop the mindset they need to approach both daily tasks and long-term goals with the confidence of a person who truly deserves the success for which they strive. Most of these tips are fairly intuitive, yet may not have occurred to some people. A lack of confidence tends to do that—it replaces our best thinking abilities with an unfortunate lack of insight.

The first tip that we are going to discuss revolves around the need to look realistically at our faults. As stated above, everyone has them. Yet rarely are your faults as bad as you might think. They can often be overcome, and sometimes they can even be transformed into strengths. It is important to recognize this if one is to develop a truly confident mindset.

The second tip that we are going to discuss should sound familiar to most people—daily affirmations. Some may have heard of this concept before, yet refused to try it because they believed it sounded hokey. The truth, however, is that they can be incredibly beneficial. One only needs to remember a few certain rules for how they are to be done, which we will examine in detail.

The third tip revolves around action. The actions we take while exhibiting a certain mindset will often help to reinforce our way of thinking. When our way of thinking is one of confidence, this reinforcement becomes crucial in not only developing but also maintaining the mindset one needs to achieve success. As such, this chapter will examine the ways in which doing just a little bit each day to achieve your goals can bolster your self-esteem and your belief that you can achieve success if you simply continue to forge ahead on the path that you have begun to set for yourself.

The fourth chapter will cover the need to realize your strengths. This may seem rudimentary, and you may wonder why it has been left until after daily action has already been taken to achieve success. The reason is simple—most people who lack self-confidence will not be aware of their own strengths until they have utilized those strengths to achieve tangible results. Once you have begun your daily affirmations and begun to engage in successful actions, it will be easier for you to look back on what has worked and what has not.

Finally, we will examine the need to track your progress in terms of your personal development. This is more difficult than it sounds. Building confidence is not like building muscle; you cannot look at a chart every day to see how much better you performed than the day before. Or can you? There are certain ways in which you can look back on how much confidence you have built since you have adopted the preceding steps, and this will help to further reinforce the notion that these seemingly simple methods can achieve great results with enough effort.

Through all things, never forget that there is a difference between confidence and cockiness. Confidence is not about telling people that you are better than them or that you are meant for better things. It is about learning how to become content with who you are so that you are more able to grow into the person that you are meant to be. It may seem frightening, but the results are well worth the effort.

Chapter 1. Assess Faults Realistically

Those who lack self-confidence can probably compose a thorough list of their faults without giving the matter much thought. Such self-debasing thoughts might sound similar to some of the following:

"I'm fat."/"I'm ugly."

"I always lose jobs."

"I never get asked out."

"I've never been married."

"I've never had kids."

"I got passed over for another promotion."

Of the preceding statements, guess how many are indicative that a person is meant for failure. In fact, take a wild guess at how many of the above statements indicate problems that are insurmountable in any way, shape or form.

If you guessed "none of them," then you're on the right track.

The above statements are not faults in one's personality, nor are they omens that a person is not fit to achieve success. They are merely unhealthy ways of thinking that set a person up for failure again and again by constantly reinforcing the idea that they are not meant for anything else.

It may be surprising to hear this, but these sorts of self-loathing condemnations of one's own character are actually something of a defense mechanism. Many people have trouble admitting that they are standing in their own way, and so they construct the notion that they are uniquely deficient as a means of avoiding the true problem at hand. A more realistic version of the above statements might read as follows:

"I eat more than I need to."/"I undervalue my hygiene."

"I underperform at work."

"I wait for my love interests to come to me."

"I do not stay in committed relationships."

"I am afraid to raise a family."

"I let my colleagues steal the spotlight at work."

Each of these revised statements presents a possible source of the problems listed at the beginning of the chapter, except that in this case, the speaker has admitted that the source of the problem might be their way of thinking. This takes the victimization out of the problem and transforms it into something that can be overcome with a fundamental shift in one's mindset.

Having established the benefits of assessing one's fault in a realistic manner, the question becomes how this can be done by someone who is prone to casting themselves in an unrealistically negative light. The answer is simpler than you might think. You must start by the problems that you wish to overcome, and simply try to determine how positive actions or a more confident mindset might help to overcome the problem.

In order to demonstrate how this might be done, let us take a look at the above pairs of statements and see what changes need to be made to reach a realistic fault assessment.

The first statement revolves around a person who perceives themselves as fat or ugly. In the revised statement, they do not attribute this to some sort of genetic fault but rather their own actions. They are not overweight because they are simply unlucky, but rather because they sometimes overeat. Overeating can sometimes be an addictive behavior, and like many addictions may be adopted to fill a void by supplementing a lack of positive emotional stimuli with an easy source of instant gratification. Others who are not comfortable with their looks may sometimes undervalue their hygiene, not shaving or brushing their teeth as often as a person whose confidence drives them to look their best. This is similar to the manner in which abuse victims will often go days without showering due to depression.

The problem with self-debasement when it comes to problems with one's self-image is that the issue becomes cyclical. A person feels as if their looks are subpar, and so they begin to slack on the upkeep of their appearance. This then reinforces the same negative thought process to which they had fallen prey before. On the other hand, when they find a simple way of improving their looks, their confidence will grow and they will reinforce the desire to continue this behavior. They must simply assess the cause of the fault, and the rest will follow suit.

The second statement and the last statement are somewhat connected. In one, the speaker is concerned that they are not able to hold a job very long. The counterpoint to this is that they might underperform at work, which is the true cause for their generally brief periods of employment. In the other statement, the speaker feels as if their performance is up to par, but that others have received credit for their achievements in the form of promotions. While it is possible that they are not realistically assessing the quality of their performance, it is also possible that they have simply allowed their colleagues to steal the spotlight for their achievements.

In both of these statements, a realistic assessment of the fault at hand is relatively easy to perform. In the first case, the person feels wronged for having been fired from jobs at which they did not perform as well as they should have. While the person may lack confidence in their performance abilities, they clearly do not lack a sense of entitlement. Otherwise, they would not feel as if they deserved to keep a job when they had not worked very hard at it to begin with. This demonstrates the strange manner in which a lack of confidence in one's own performance abilities might actually result in a type of grandiosity. As previously mentioned, this grandiose way of thinking is merely a defense mechanism that keeps people from performing a more honest assessment of the problem at hand.

In the other job-related statement, the person is concerned with the fact that their colleagues appear to receive promotions while they are stuck in the same position. Again, it is possible that they suffer from the same problem as the person above, and simply have not underperformed to the extent that they have lost their job. On the other hand, they might be a dedicated worker who simply does not have the confidence to outshine their coworkers.

Perhaps a colleague has taken credit for their achievements, and they did not have the self-respect to stand up for themselves. It is also possible that their colleague simply had the foresight to ask their boss about upcoming promotions, while they did not. Many do not think about the fact that promotions are not always handed out to the most senior employee. Sometimes, a person has to inquire about potential openings. If a person does not feel that they are worthy of a promotion, they will not be as likely to ask.

In either of these cases, the person in question must simply have enough confidence to earn the respect they feel they deserve. They must be confident in their performance abilities, bringing this confidence to the table in all of their work-related endeavors. If a person is looking for advancement opportunities, they must be confident enough to inquire about them rather than waiting for their employer to make an offer. Those who are most likely to succeed in business are those who choose to pursue opportunities on their own merit.

Three of the statements at the beginning of this chapter pertain to relationships and long-term family goals. The first is spoken by a person who never gets asked on dates. The problem here is simple, and can be addressed quite easily: they wait to be asked, rather than asking themselves. Much like the employee who sits around and waits for a promotion, this person has become dissatisfied and malcontent because they have not been offered something that they do not have the confidence to simply request. They must assess this side of the problem, rather than allowing themselves to become a victim of their own inaction.

The next two statements concern people who blame their lack of self-confidence on the fact that they have not yet become married or had children. Often, the problem here will be similar to that of the person who never goes on dates. The person in question does not pursue a committed relationship, and therefore is given no opportunity to advance their family life. Then, there are those who are in a committed relationship, but fear taking the next step. Perhaps they are worried that the person that are dating will not say "yes" if they propose. If they are married, then perhaps they fear their abilities as a future parent. Since they have not realistically assessed this aspect of the problem, they remain mired in self-pity and low self-esteem, feeling as if they have not achieved what they want out of life.

This is where confidence might truly come in handy. When a person truly feels that they are ready to take the next step in life, sometimes they must simply dive right in. A realistic assessment of their problems might reveal that the major roadblock preventing them from getting married or having kids is that they have simply been too afraid. Maybe they are afraid of rejection, or of the increased responsibilities associated with becoming a spouse or parent. Either way, they must realize the issue before they can overcome it.

Of course, a truly realistic assessment might also reveal the opposite problem. Perhaps there is another reason they have not felt able to propose to their loved one or suggest the notion of moving forward with their relationship and becoming a family. In some cases, the harsh truth may be that the relationship doesn't work. If this is the case, they will often find that they do not lack the confidence to propose, but rather the confidence to break off the relationship. It takes a lot of self-respect to decide not to settle for something that is not working, and this often holds people back when combined with the fear of being alone. Anyone who has assessed the source of their relationship issues and determined that the relationship is not worth continuing must have the self-respect to break things off, as well as the confidence to trust that doing so will not mean that they are doomed to be single forever.

Each of the above issues can be solved through confidence and self-respect, but not before the person has taken a long, hard look at the faults that underlie their various problems. Whether the problems you have identified in your own life are affecting your work, your relationships, or simply your overall self-image, you must understand why you think this way before you can determine the areas of your life in which confidence is most vital to success and personal development.

Chapter 2. Do Daily Affirmations

At some point in your life, you have probably seen a movie or television program in which a character stands in front of a mirror, stares themselves in the face, and repeats a list of positive affirmations meant to get them through a date, a job interview, or possibly even just the beginning of the day. This is a real tool that many people use to build confidence daily, but some shy away from this method because its portrayal in popular media has led some to think of it as just another tacky stereotype that couldn't possibly work for them.

But the truth is that it absolutely can work. The use of daily affirmations has improved the lives of many. If a person ever tells you that they did not receive any benefit from using daily affirmations, ask them how many times they tried before quitting. The odds are that they will give you a relatively low number. Some may even state that they tried repeating affirmations only a single time before giving up because they did not feel any different.

What many do not understand about affirmations is that they take time. When you first start doing your affirmations in the mirror every morning, they will probably feel strange. Most people are not accustomed to verbally talking themselves up in general, let alone while speaking to themselves in the mirror.

The mirror aspect is another roadblock for some people. After all, if you have low self-confidence to begin with, then it is a safe bet that you aren't always happy with the person staring back at you from the other side of the glass. To stand there and compliment that person will feel odd, and possibly even wrong.

The other major problem that some will encounter when attempting to start their daily affirmations is that there is no perfect list of affirmations to give. Many will not know what to say. They will want to find something that is as complimentary as it needs to be without feeling like a lie. Again, the inherent problem with this is that those who suffer from low self-esteem will not likely have much confidence in any affirmations they choose.

Believe it or not, these problems are fundamentally related to the very reasons that affirmations work in the first place. As a person repeats their affirmations every day, they will slowly but surely begin to reinforce those ideas in their mind. They will begin to believe them, and after a time they may even look forward to starting their morning. As they grow more accustomed to speaking to themselves in the mirror, they might also find themselves growing more comfortable with the face they see in the glass. Once their affirmations have reached their full potential, the person in question will reach a point at which they might change their affirmations every day to suit their specific goals. Having reached a point of contentment with themselves and the face staring back at them from the mirror, they will be more inclined to believe any affirmation they devise.

The key is to start small. The following are some of the basic affirmations often recommended to people who are in need of a confidence boost:

> "People love me."

"I deserve to be happy."

"I am unique."

"I forgive myself for past mistakes."

"I am in charge of my own success."

"I am important to those around me."

"Today will be a good day."

These affirmations will be difficult for those who are not actually inclined to believe these statements. The key to turning these around is to focus on simple rewordings that will make them more believable. As such, try to change just one or two words. A revised version of the above list might read as follows:

"I *can* be loved."

"I *can* achieve happiness."

"I *can* become unique."

"I *can* forgive myself for past mistakes."

"I *can* take charge of my own success."

"I *can* become important to those around me."

"Today *can* be a good day."

Note that the word "can" has been italicized in each of these revisions. This one word makes each of the previous affirmations sound less absolute, and therefore more believable. It is a truly simple change, but it can make a world of difference to the person who is attempting to state these affirmations without falling prey to doubt and self-pity. As time goes on, you might find yourself replacing these revised affirmations with their originals. However, when first starting out, it is simply easier to utilize affirmations that express confidence in the sheer possibility of achieving happiness and success, rather than trying to convince yourself that such things are indisputable promises that will accompany you every day.

The other benefit of utilizing the word "can" when first beginning daily affirmations is that it causes each affirmative statement to issue a subtle call to action. There is an implied ending to every affirmation that contains this word:

"I *can* be loved, but only if I am *open* to love."

"I *can* achieve happiness, but only if I *try*."

"I *can* become unique, but only if I am *honest* about my strengths."

"I *can* become important to those around me, <u>but only if I truly *care*</u>."

"I *can* take charge of my own success, <u>but only if I *choose* to do so</u>."

"I *can* become important to those around me, <u>but only if I am *willing*</u>."

"Today *can* be a good day, <u>but only if I *make* it one</u>."

Not only will the word "can" allow you to approach these affirmations with more of an open mind, but the implied endings to each affirmation will drive you to pursue actions and ways of thinking that make the affirmations easier to believe. The promise that today can be a good day will make you want to do everything in your power to make it as good as possible. The promise that you can be loved will convince you to remain open to love. You might even see that your days have been good and that you have been loved all along. You simply failed to see it because you were mired in a morass of low confidence and self-doubt.

Once you have begun to grow accustomed to these affirmations (to the point that you no longer need the word "can" in order to believe them), you can begin to alter your affirmation to suit the needs of the day. Perhaps you have a date or a job interview, and you need to tell yourself that things will go well. Perhaps you have a troublesome family event such as a funeral, and you need to tell yourself that you will not break down. Perhaps you are undergoing an unexplained emotional disturbance, and you simply need to tell yourself that you will make it through the next twenty-four hours. No matter what type of affirmation you need, you will have increased your confidence to the point that you are able to believe whatever you need to tell yourself.

When creating your affirmations, bear in mind what you learned in the first chapter. You must have a realistic understanding of the faults that you are trying to correct, or else you may devise affirmations to boost your confidence in areas where it is not needed. You also want to be realistic in general when writing your affirmations. If you come up with something specific and crazy, such as "I will win the lottery," then the likely failure of this statement to prove true will ultimately reinforce in the back of your mind that it is not worth your time to continue doing affirmations in the future.

Also remember that even the most realistic affirmations should not be seen as psychic predictions. You may do daily affirmations that concern your ability to achieve success, or simply the notion that "today can/will be a good day." But the fact of life is that people sometimes fail, and they sometimes have bad days. This does not mean, however, that they will not achieve success in one form or another the following day, or that good days never follow the bad ones.

The goal of affirmations is not to promise oneself constant success and happiness with no interruptions whatsoever. The primary goal is to simply reinforce the notion that confidence can yield great rewards for those who are open to them. Don't skip your daily affirmations simply because the previous day could have gone better. The sun just might shine a little brighter today, but only if you maintain the confident mindset required to let the sunshine in. If you give up on your affirmations because of one minor upset, it will be as if a dark cloud has forced its way into your life.

Remember what was said earlier about the fact that many will likely find that the love and happiness they hope to achieve through affirmations have likely been present all along, but were simply overshadowed by a cloud of doubt and self-pity. Confidence and open-mindedness will cause this cloud to disperse, allowing you to see the light in your life. If saying a few brief affirmations every morning can help you to achieve this confidence, then you have no excuse for not taking a few seconds out of your day to try this simple yet effective method.

Chapter 3. Build a Little Each Day

So, you have assessed your faults and you have begun doing affirmations each day to reaffirm your self-worth and boost your confidence. But maybe you're now in a rut. Maybe your affirmations are taking longer to work for you than you expected, or maybe they were boosting your confidence for a while but you find your self-esteem is beginning to plateau. Where do you go from here? How do you keep yourself going strong?

The answer is actually fairly intuitive, yet you would be amazed at how many people fail to arrive at this solution on their own: you must begin to give yourself a *reason* to be confident.

You must begin to fulfill your goals, no matter what they may be.

This is where some people may get defiant. They might point out that they've attempted to achieve their goals in the past, but were met with failure and possibly even derision. That's how they got into this mess of low self-esteem and diminishing self-worth to begin with!

If that sounds like you, then maybe we should take a look at *how* you went about trying to achieve your goals in the past. Let's say your goal is to get a new job, or even just to secure a better position within your current place of employment. Did you try to shoot for the stars, immediately applying for the position you wanted without first taking any steps to improve your credentials and make yourself more appealing to the employer? Perhaps you are happy with your current position, and you are tying your self-confidence to more basic goals such as getting married and having kids. How have you gone about trying to attain these goals? Have you proposed to your previous mates too soon? Have you tried to settle with the first person with whom you crossed paths, failing to take into account whether or not you were actually well-suited to tie the knot with one another?

Trying to force your goals into fruition is not the key to attaining a confident mindset. If anything, it is a surefire way to ensure that you continue to value your confidence in your true worth, even when you do manage to achieve your goals. If you truly wish to feel at peace with your achievements, then you must earn them. This does not have to be done overnight, in leaps and bounds. It can be done in smaller steps, and this might even be the preferred method for those who are in the midst of trying to develop a confident mindset.

The first thing you're going to want to do is to set the goals themselves. You have technically already done this in the first two chapters, even if you were not completely cognizant of the fact. Even those who feel lost, believing themselves not to have any life goals, have discovered their true goals without even realizing it. When you tried to realistically assess your faults, you were looking primarily at the character defects which stood in the way of getting what you want. This means that, even if it was on a subconscious level, you have had some semblance of an idea regarding your true goals all along. You then reinforced these goals in the second chapter, when you told yourself through your affirmations about what type of person you wanted to be. Even if your affirmations were based around strengths you already possess and achievements you have already made, you can bet dollars to donuts that you wouldn't have focused on those particular strengths and achievements unless they tied into your overall life goals.

Once you have looked back at these earlier steps in order to discover the goals that must be set in place to achieve happiness, it is time to begin building confidence that you can achieve these goals with enough effort. Since you will build more and more confidence over time if you do just a little bit each day to further the advancement of these goals, it is best to break them up into several smaller steps. Instead of one major achievement that feels as if it is far out of reach, located in the vast and seemingly unattainable future, you will have numerous milestones that you can achieve in a relatively short amount of time.

For instance, let's suppose that your primary goal right now is to better yourself through physical fitness. Maybe you want to lose a fairly standard amount of weight, such as twenty or thirty pounds. Since losing weight can take a long time, you may become frustrated if you are constantly looking toward the end goal. You might weigh yourself every day, becoming more and more frustrated with every day that the scale stays the same. You'd be amazed at how many people give up within weeks or even days because they fall into this trap.

The problem in this case is that not only does losing weight take a long time, but the scale is not completely reliable. Weight fluctuates, and one or two more pounds on the scale might be chalked up to water weight rather than fat. In addition, many people will gain muscle while they are exercising, which tends to skew the numbers due to the fact that muscle weighs more than fat.

These are the same issues that you may want to keep in mind when setting smaller goals. If you are lifting weights in addition to cardiovascular exercise, you might look at how much more you are able to lift over the course of the week, whether in regard to the amount of weight lifted or the number of repetitions. You might try going for slightly longer periods of time on the treadmill, even as little as a minute or two each day. This will allow you to see that you are getting into shape, even if the scale does not always display the numbers you want to see.

Now let's take a look at your relationship goals. Needless to say, the first major roadblock in trying to build a relationship is going to be simply meeting people with compatible mindsets. But even that can be broken down into the smaller goal of meeting people in general and then getting to know them. If you are notoriously inept when it comes to social situations, then you are going to have to start by simply putting yourself out there. You do not necessarily have to start by meeting people with whom you think you'd like to develop a relationship. You might start by simply meeting people in public places such as the grocery store. Try to spark up a conversation with a stranger. It might not always go well, but bear in mind that this can be partly attributed to the simple fact that many people might not be expecting a conversation when they are out shopping. However, when it does go well, you will find yourself becoming a little more confident in your ability to come out of your shell and meet people.

Once you have learned that you are capable of meeting people, you might start trying to approach people with whom you think you might be compatible. Try to get a phone number or two. Even an email address is fine. Then, try to turn this into a date. You do not have to hang your hat on the first date—it is not indicative of whether or not you are capable of building a relationship, but rather simply whether or not you are compatible with the person in question. You will build much more confidence if you act like yourself over the course of the first few dates, rather than trying to put on a mask that you will not be able to maintain if things blossom into a more serious relationship.

If you do find yourself in a relationship, trying to build upon smaller goals may begin to become a slightly more difficult task. There is not necessarily a set of smaller milestones that lead to marriage or children. That said, one can still build daily confidence in their relationship through the fulfillment of smaller tasks. Try to do something for your loved one every day. Doing things for others can be a surprisingly beneficial confidence builder, especially when trying to reassure yourself that you are worthy of becoming someone's lifelong partner in matrimony. Every once in a while, try to set a somewhat larger goal to do something as a couple that you have not done before. Once you have the confidence to propose, you might build confidence as a future parent by fulfilling smaller tasks to make yourself feel like a responsible person. Again, try to be generous when possible. This will do wonders for your self-worth, not only as a potential spouse or parent, but as a person in general.

Finally, let's examine your career goals. It is not unusual to want a better job, but it is not the kind of thing that people just earn overnight without putting a bit of work in. Your daily goals are largely going to revolve around building your credentials and your overall appeal as an employee. Think back on the advice mentioned earlier in regards to physical fitness. If you just get through a little more work each day, you will slowly and steadily establish yourself as a more worthwhile employee. You might also try to build your relationship with your boss, starting with simple greetings and trying to build into longer conversations.

Like all of the above goals, building your career prospects will not be achieved with immediacy, nor will you always be successful. Perhaps you try to spark up a conversation with your boss on a day that he or she is simply not feeling that social. Perhaps you try to become more efficient, but in the process you overestimate your limitations and accidentally take on a larger workload than one person can handle alone. These things happen; do not fret over it, but simply try to stand tall and keep on striving to do your best. Even setbacks such as these can boost your confidence, as they will teach you that you are capable of getting back on the horse with perseverance and aplomb.

If you are not working for another person, but rather trying to start your own venture, then you will still want to take it a step at a time. Develop an idea, and shop it around to friends, acquaintances, and possibly even strangers you meet at the mall. See how it is perceived by people. Then begin developing your plan on a step-by-step basis. You do not have to become an entrepreneur overnight. Do whatever it takes to build confidence in your ideas, and in the process you will become the type of person who is capable of achieving success in such ventures.

The benefit to setting such small goals and simply building upon them each day is that they not only reinforce your confidence in your abilities, but they actually reward you for every small achievement. Before, when you looked at some big plan you had for yourself that you had not achieved, you may have been stuck in a morass of low self-confidence and possibly even sheer depression. However, these smaller milestones pay off massively every time one of them reaches completion. They brain rewards people with dopamine when a feeling of success is attained. This leads to happiness that, even in short bursts, can help a person to achieve a truly confident mindset over time.

The brain's reward system is nothing to sneeze at. Finding out how to exploit it is a major part of developing a confident mindset. Once you have begun building on small achievements on a daily basis, you will be well on your way to developing confidence in your strengths and in your abilities.

Chapter 4. Realize Your Strengths

If you're reading these chapters in order, and stopping to heed the advice of each one before continuing, then you are now at a point at which you have begun to take action. At this point, you should be building more confidence than ever, especially if you are learning from the occasional mistake. But some of the inevitable slip-ups you will encounter when pursuing a more confident mindset may also be planting seeds of self-doubt. If this has happened to you, then this chapter should help you to get over the hump. If it has not happened to you, then you will still benefit from looking over the recent actions you have taken and assessing the strengths that have come to light through your achievements, no matter how big or how small.

It may seem odd to you that this chapter does not immediately follow the first chapter on realistically assessing your faults; however, there is a reason for this. Those who truly lack confidence will not be as able to realize their strengths as someone who has been given a chance to see them shine through the fruits of their labors. When taking daily action to build upon your achievements, you will not just gain general confidence in your abilities to succeed and become a more well-rounded human being, but you will actually gain confidence that is relatable to the specific skillsets you possess— and probably have possessed throughout your entire life, even if you weren't in a position to let yourself realize it.

There are numerous character assets that might be aiding you in your endeavors. You may discover some that pertain specifically to your special skills and abilities, but the following are some of the most basic attributes that those with low self-confidence are often surprised to discover in themselves. These include:

- Perseverance
- Generosity
- Kindness/Gentleness
- Intelligence
- Resourcefulness
- Creativity
- Charm/Magnetism

The importance of these attributes, as well as any others that may have come to light through your achievements, cannot be overstated. Taking a look at each in turn will grant you an idea of the powerful and worthwhile person that you really are, and will reaffirm the notion that you must have confidence in yourself in order to bring these assets to the forefront in all of your endeavors. Not only will it be healthy for your self-esteem, but those around you will benefit from seeing you become stronger and more self-assured.

First, let's take a look at perseverance. Maybe you don't see this quality in yourself, but bear in mind that you have made it through three chapters leading up to this one. In order to persevere, a person often needs other character attributes such as open-mindedness. Through your willingness to take advice and develop your character, you have shown all of these abilities. At times, it has probably seemed more difficult than it should. You may have doubted yourself because you thought that you did not deserve the confidence you were trying to develop. You may have endured setbacks when you suffered from a particularly bad day that made you lose faith in your daily affirmations, or when you attempted to better yourself through the achievement of simple daily goals only to find yourself facing unexpected failure due to circumstances beyond your control (or worse, completely within your control). Yet here you are, still willing to do what it takes to develop the confident mindset necessary to your success. It may not seem like much, but you deserve a pat on the back for it.

Next, let's take a look at generosity. In the last chapter, it was noted that your daily actions might revolve around doing good deeds for others. This may have seemed selfish if you were doing it primarily to further your relationship or your career, but ask yourself one simple question: Did it feel selfish afterward? Almost definitely not. Generosity of character is important. It builds confidence by reminding you that you are a decent human being, and that you deserve any good things which might come your way.

If you succeeded in building the attribute of generosity, then you likely exhibited your innermost kindness and gentleness in the process. Even when not actively performing good deeds in the service of your fellow human beings, the odds are that these qualities are still present in all that you do. There are some who react to their own lack of self-confidence by wearing a mask of grandiosity, or by maliciously taking their self-hatred out on those around them. If you are not one of those people, then you are to be commended. You can move forward with increased confidence in your likelihood of success, because you know that people will see the good in you and that you will be rewarded for it, no matter how much effort it might take.

You may have also recently discovered that you are much more intelligent than you once thought. All too often, those who lack confidence will reinforce their negative beliefs by reminding themselves how stupid or insufficient they think they are, but this is not true of most people. Regardless of IQ, just about everyone in the world possesses one form of intelligence or another. Maybe a person does not possess the book smarts to become a doctor or a lawyer, but they can take apart a car engine and put it back together without even thinking about it. Maybe a person does not possess any particular vocational skills, but is highly adept at reading people and responding to their needs. You may not often think about it, but these are all forms of intelligence. They all take a level of intuition that should prove to anyone who possesses such abilities that they are far from stupid. Don't get caught up in the grades you made in college, and do not focus on the one time you spoke without thinking in a social situation. Such instances might have been guidelines for areas in which you might wish to improve, but they were not signs of overall stupidity.

Intelligence is often accompanied by resourcefulness. If you have been taking small steps to improve your abilities in the workplace, then you have likely come to realize that you possess this skill in abundance. When you think about it, you have actually exhibited resourcefulness in every step of developing your confident mindset. This book may have provided a few ideas and examples, but you were ultimately the one who had to look at your own life and assess the areas which needed improving. You were the one who had to devise a set of daily affirmations that would best fit your needs. You were the one who had to figure out which daily actions you could take to improve your confidence and your life in general. If this doesn't sound like resourcefulness to you, then you may be operating under a restrictive definition of the word. Being resourceful doesn't mean that you have to be MacGyver, able to disarm a missile with a paperclip or make landmines out of pine cones (yes, he really did that). Being resourceful simply means that you are able to make the most of what you have, which is integral to the development of confidence and general contentment with oneself.

Much like resourcefulness and intelligence, creativity and resourcefulness go hand in hand. In order to make the most with what you have, you may sometimes have to be creative. This is especially true when trying to increase your efficiency in the workplace, or organize a date with a prospective loved one while on a budget.

Of course, much like intelligence, there are numerous forms of creativity. You may be artistically creative, able to write, draw, play music, or simply entertain those around you with a creative sense of humor. You might be creative in ways that apply more to your line of work, able to devise innovative solutions to problems that your company is experiencing. This is one of the more important strengths for you to realize, as you will benefit both yourself and those around you if you are able to build up enough confidence to let your creativity shine forth uninhibited. Those with low self-confidence sometimes have trouble expressive unfettered creativity, because they fear the rejection of their ideas. If you can overcome this fear, then you are much more likely to succeed in most of your endeavors.

The last of the general strengths listed above are charm and magnetism. They are essentially the same thing, although charm can be affected whereas magnetism is more of a natural quality. Either way, you would have been most likely to realize this strength if trying to meet people in public places (as was recommended for those seeking improvements in their personal relationships) or when trying to get to know your boss (as was suggested for those seeking to further their careers). Out of all of the general strengths listed in this chapter, charm can take the longest to realize in oneself due to the fact that it tends to improve as confidence is built. Nonetheless, you may have been surprised when noting certain improvements to find that charm and magnetism might actually come much easier for you than you had previously realized. The more you bring this skill to the table in your daily interactions with others, the more you will find that a confident mindset begins to naturally develop within you.

Not all of the above strengths are going to apply to every person with equal measure, but most will discover they possess each of these attributes to one degree or another. Rare is the person who is incapable of persevering through difficult times—if such people were common, most of us would not survive past high school. Most people also possess generosity and kindness, even if they do not always exhibit those qualities to the best of their abilities. Intelligence, resourcefulness, and creativity also tend to reside in most people to varying degrees. And charm might be a skill that one develops over time, but most people have a naturally magnetic personality that they simply have not expressed due to a lack of confidence in themselves.

Of course, these are not the grand total of possible strengths that you may realize when developing a confident mindset. You may have more specific traits that others find beneficial, traits that adhere primarily to your choice of profession or to the manner in which you form and maintain relationships with others. You might be good with animals, excellent with finances, or appreciative of family values. The third item in that sentence may not sound like a strength, but your family probably likes it. And if it's something that you like about yourself, then realizing that will make you just a little bit stronger.

The above advice isn't simply about making the most of your innate abilities as a human being, but about appreciating those abilities to grow content and build your self-love. This will be a vital component in not only developing a confident mindset, but ensuring that you have a reason to maintain it for quite some time to come.

Chapter 5. Track Your Progress

In the introduction to this book, it was stated that building confidence is not like building muscle, that it is not as simple as looking at a chart to see if you are lifting more weight than you were the day before. This was followed, however, by the reassurance that tracking your progress in regard to confidence building is actually much easier than you might be inclined to think.

The major key to tracking your progress is to do it often. You may wish to do it every day at first, preferably at night while you are winding down and getting ready for bed. Go over the happenings of the day in your head and assess any major events or interactions with others that had a notable impact on your thinking, whether the impact in question was positive or negative.

In fact, while you can easily do this in your head, you might consider keeping a journal or two. You can take notes in one journal, or you can keep one by your bed and the other with you at all times. The one by your bed will be for nightly inventory, while the one you keep with you will be for jotting down notes on anything that might influence your confidence throughout the day. When you attempt to track your progress at night, this smaller journal will make it easier to perform an honest assessment of your confidence throughout the day. As for the nightly inventory, you might want to jot down the following questions and answer them each night:

1. What made me feel a lack of confidence today?
2. How well did I handle this damage to my confidence levels?
3. What increased my confidence today?
4. Was I overly confident or cocky as a result of these increases?
5. Was my confidence directly responsible for any of my achievements today?
6. Was a lack of confidence directly responsible for any of my mistakes?
7. What faults have I identified today, or which were most prevalent?
8. Which strengths have I identified today?
9. What could I have done today in order to improve?
10. What can I work on tomorrow in terms of thoughts or specific actions?

This list of questions is designed to help you engage in a process of self-reflection in order to continue building your confidence based upon each day's performance. It will help you to assess your faults and realize your strengths while pinpointing specific situations in which it is difficult for you to maintain your confidence (as well as situations in which it is the easiest).

As you engage in this process of self-reflection more and more, you might eventually get to the point where it does not require as much effort. You might be able to easily process this information mentally, rather than writing it all down in a journal. In addition, you may very well grow to the point that you no longer need to do it every day. As time goes on, you will be more cognizant of your performance at work or in social situations, and you will recognize with more immediacy how this relates to your overall level of confidence. Even when you reach this point, however, you might consider continuing to take this written inventory at least once a week, revising the questions to meet that standard. This will help you to continue being honest with yourself, rather than simply shrugging it off and assuming that you have done your best. With the exception of particularly good days or particularly bad ones, it is quite rare that you will not have anything to write for each and every question on the list.

One of the best things about this step in your development of a confident mindset is that it simultaneously manages to build upon the steps elaborated in the previous chapters while also improving your ability to follow them. After all, there would be little point in this process of self-reflection if you had not begun taking actions to improve your confidence. Otherwise, you would not have nearly as much inventory to take, nor would you be able to do so with nearly as much honesty. At the same time, it will be easier to follow the advice of the previous chapters once you have reached this step in your personal development. Your ability to honestly and realistically track your daily progress will make further attempts at confidence development more meaningful.

While there are a number of questions in the list, they can basically be boiled down into two types. There are those which assess the areas in which you need the most improvement, and there are those which assess your strengths (as well as what needs to be done to build these further). It is important to be equally honest when answering both of these types of questions if you are to develop your confidence to the fullest extent. If you do not honestly assess each moment in the day that proved difficult in maintaining your confidence, then you cannot hope to identify such situations more easily in the future. On the other hand, if you do not honestly assess each moment in the day during which your confidence was at its highest, then you will not be able to recreate such moments in order to bring out your strengths on a daily basis.

This step may not be as complicated as some of those which precede it, but it might feel overbearing when you are first starting out. No matter how much progress you have made, looking back on every day and going over your performance in terms of confidence building can feel like a daunting task. It is also easy to forget to do this, since it is done at the end of the day when you are likely tired and ready to go to sleep. As such, try to do it while you are still fairly awake, perhaps right before you brush your teeth, shower, or whatever you may do as part of your nightly routine. You can then reflect further upon your answers to each question while you go about your business in preparation for a night of slumber.

Above all, however, do not forget that you are tracking your progress with the express intention of making further progress in the days to come. This should prove to be a primary motivating factor in your development of a confident mindset, as it will remind you that there is always progress to be made. Human beings never peak unless they let themselves. You can continue improve throughout the rest of your life if you simply track your progress daily and continue to pay attention to the lessons that you learn every day.

Conclusion

Now that you have begun to follow the above five steps, you have taken gigantic leaps toward the development of a confident mindset. There is now only one thing you need to remember:

> You are never done.

This is not to say that you should not be proud of the progress that you have made, but personal development is something that human beings engage in throughout the entirety of their lives. You may be feeling pretty confident right now, but the same things that used to eat away at your self-worth are still out there, and many of them still reside within your own mind.

That said, you are certainly not to lose hope at this juncture. Let's just take a look back on what you have learned so far, and how you can benefit from continuing to follow the course of action that you have learned throughout the process of reading this book.

First, you learned how to realistically assess your faults. By now, you should be an ace at this. You should know how to tell the difference between identifying problems or character defects that need to be addressed, and the sheer self-debasement in which you may have been engaging before. Now that you are more fully aware of the difference between the two, you can continue to identify key problems in your behaviors and your way of thinking that may be standing in the way between you and true happiness. This will become important whenever you encounter problems in the future that make it tempting to look down on yourself. Remember that "failure" is just a word. It is not a state of being unless you succumb to it.

Second, you learned about the benefits of daily affirmations. You learned that they can sometimes be difficult, especially when your affirmations are not in line with your true beliefs regarding your character. Nonetheless, you have hopefully grown by now to the extent that you are not only able to believe these affirmations, but to alter them to meet the needs of the day ahead. While it had been suggested that you do them early in the morning, perhaps you have found that it sometimes helps you to do them again at lunch time, or even right before bed. Either way, you have taken a valuable tool and found a way to make it work for you. This is integral to your growth as a confident and self-assured human being.

Third, you have begun taking action every day to behave in a manner that will increase your overall confidence. Whether you are trying to better yourself through physical fitness, advance your career, or simply get out there and meet people, you have learned that you are capable of finding ways to better yourself on a daily basis. Not only should this have increased your confidence, but it should have benefitted your life in countless other ways depending upon the specific daily actions that you have chosen to take.

Fourth, you have learned to identify your strengths based upon the true character that shone through over the course of your daily confidence building. Not only have you built some of these strengths as a result of your efforts to develop a confident mindset, but you have also discovered which of these strengths were within you long before you chose to bolster your self-esteem. You have learned to bring these strengths to the table whenever possible, and you have seen the benefits that the character attributes at your disposal have had upon your confidence, as well as the positive impact that these assets have had on the lives of those around you.

Finally, you have learned the benefits of self-reflection. You have taken a bit of time out each week or even each day in order to look back on your actions and your thought processes to determine what types of actions or situations might pose a threat to your growing confidence, and you have reasonably assessed your performance in terms of keeping your confidence up and facing life's problems with assurance and self-esteem. This has no doubt helped you with the above steps, as it has helped you to assess both your strengths and your weaknesses while revising your affirmations and developing ideas regarding what action might be taken each day in order to continue your journey of self-improvement.

You might have noticed that the above paragraph describes the fifth lesson in a somewhat cyclical manner. This is because none of these steps are a one-time deal. While following the lessons learned in this book will help you to develop a more confident mindset, you will need to continue heeding this advice if such a mindset is to be maintained. Otherwise, you risk falling into the same patterns of thoughts and behavior in which you were mired before you began reading. This is not good for your confidence, and it is certainly not good for your well-being.

Some people might find this idea scary. No one wants to be told that they can never become perfect, or that they will have to keep working in order to achieve what seems to come so naturally to certain other people. Do not engage in this type of thinking. First, remember that the more you follow these steps, the less they will feel like work. Second, approach the issue with enthusiasm. You should be excited that you are never done, because it means that you have the opportunity to continue growing as a person throughout the rest of your life. This is a wonderful gift.

Through confidence, you can achieve what you want out of life. You just have to be honest with yourself, open to the idea of changing what you need to, and willing to perform the necessary steps in order to become a more confident person. When you find yourself facing each day with less fear and more self-assurance, you will be glad that you made the effort.

www.ingramcontent.com/pod-product-compliance
Lightning Source LLC
Chambersburg PA
CBHW052204110526
44591CB00012B/2077